ISBN# 978-0615707471
ISBN# 978-1624076749
Printed in the United States of America

Cover Scenes from Wayne County, Kentucky.

The old English style graves are an Appalachian tradition brought to the region by early settlers.

BURIAL TRADITIONS IN THE REGION OF THE UPPER CUMBERLAND PLATEAU.

Vaults are of three types (1) a Flat Topped Rectangular type, (2) a Coffin-shaped Capstone type, and (3) a Lean-To type.

This grave scene is from the gravesite of William Bailey Roberts born 1765, and Lidia Ponder Roberts. It is told their ancestors were likely born in England.

The Mountain Cliffs scene is called Pilot Rock, and near Pueblo in Wayne County, Kentucky, overlooking another Roberts' cemetery.

Introducing the author, Cas Roberts

Cas Roberts was born in 1950s Wayne County, Kentucky. His home of hewed logs was located on the ridge at Barrier Mountain. Transportation was by walking, horseback, or wagon. Cas had eight brothers and one sister. His first two years he walked to a one room school, ending with sixth grade and a self taught education. At thirteen, he was working the logging trade and in sawmills.

Two marriages resulted in six children. He spent over twenty six years in Indiana. Working in factories and working as a diesel mechanic. Cas relocated back to central Kentucky in nineteen ninety three and returning to the old logging trade he learn as a young boy.

Cas says "Appalachia is my roots. Growing up with old world ways and a self learned education, with hard work and determination, I have made it. My poems are about that life as I saw it. With old world ways, hard times, sad times, family, and personal experiences throughout my life times is recorded in my work."

For more information or to contact the author:
606-379-5670 cas51950@aol.com
facebook.com/cas.roberts7

Contents:

Appalachia

Carolinas to the Cumberland
Traveling horseback and wagon
Feet and wheels softly clatter
Long valleys with towering mountain tops
Majestic cliffs the eyes can see
Only eagles have a better sight
White tail deer peacefully graze and roam
"The happy hunting ground," red man said
The Cherokee called it, "home."
The pioneer man is searching for his dream
On a stream near a river
The man made his stake
For the man's service in a war
He earned his spread near and far
Mountain tops with meadows, bringing streams
Early man had reached his dreams
Rivers and streams traveling as in flight
Large boulders lined the stream
That born the name from a river
A cabin to be built in the meadow
As morning sun will bring streaks of light
While an eagle keeps a watchful eye
The little children play nearby
Appalachia man made a home
Never more will he roam
Now the mountains
Will be called his home…

Mountain Home

On a mountain in the far,
Once stood a cabin home.
A barn, where livestock open roam,
Horse wagon, parked under a cedar tree,
The sweet potato bed is just ahead.
Sugar plum tree, in the corner of a yard.
Chicken house for the eggs,
Hand churned butter milk,
Sit in a spring to cool.
Garden is planted in early spring,
For the food it will bring.
At the end of the walk,
A slatted fence with a gate,
Wood yard in the front,
Chop wood and crosscut saw,
One big black mare,
Apple and peach tree bloom in spring,
While Easter lilies line the walk.
Porch and swing to set and talk,
Kerosene lamp on a table at night,
Mother reads to children in light not bright,
Teach them to do right.
Morning does bring the sun light,
Work will be until its dusk,
Until all the chores are done.
As life was in a Mountain Home…

Mountains

From the mountains to the city,
A trail that has a terrible flight,
The sweet smell of mountain spring,
It can never leave your veins.
All concrete and carbon dioxide,
Will have no forest smell,
Just causes loss of mind, do tell.
Warm summer rain on a metal rooftop,
In a city can cause your heart to stop.
The streams of sunlight in a forest,
Never happens in a city.
Like the giant oak tree swaying in a breeze,
Just concrete buildings made with steel.
The sounds of an owl at night,
Only cars with lights so bright,
The ripple sound of a stream of water,
Will disappear in all the clatter,
Big city lights at night,
Never allow the stars to be so bright.
Just watch a glowing moon,
Disappear amongst all this clatter.
Now you wonder why this does matter.
The mountains pull at your heart,
It makes you wonder where you start.
One day you can end this restless flight,
For the mountains always pull you back.

Man

The Cherokee called it, Yamacraw,
That is a crossing on a river.
For the men's service in a war,
He made homestead near and far.
Giant boulders lines a stream,
As peaceful waters flowing into a river,
Become the name of Rock Creek.
Traveling through the Roberts hollow,
Many names would come to follow.
Sand and marbles make up the cliffs,
Red and white, as the men that came to pass.
European nations would mix his blood,
With all of mankind
The Cherokee nation,
Would become Appalachia at last,
A stronger nation was at hand.
Born from the Appalachia man.

End of Time

Old days, old ways,
Does anyone know today?
Why our ancestors chose this land?
How they worked and lived,
That built this Appalachia man.
With an ax and cross cut saws,
Hillside plows and garden hoe.
Building cabin homes with their hands,
Mules and horses, clearing fields,
How they lived off the land.
Large gardens, wild game,
It was the only food chain.
Their struggles for a reason,
To give all a better life,
Bound family and communities,
  Always help other out.
The beauty of these hills,
 The many things it is about.
As all of Appalachia will stand,
Until the End of Time!

Toy

Toys came in many shapes,
For all mountain girls and boys,
This boy had a hoop from a wagon wheel,
Twelve inch across made of steel.
Bend a U at the end of a number nine wire.
Object rolling hoop up and down hills.
Run fast and slow wire in hand,
Over rock and boulders,
On and on you go.
Pick up spinning on wire,
Doughnuts, figure eight.
What a wonderful toy,
For a mountain boy!

Mountain Life

Spring comes turning everything green.
Go to woods and earn some money,
Mountain life was no milk and honey,
You are going to see.
Bark from elm tree,
Peeled, cleaned, put in bag,
Carry out on my back.
Ginseng was very scarce.
Rattlesnakes, copperheads,
Days you find more snakes,
Than the herbs you chase.
May apple, bloodroot, wild ginger,
All herbs mankind needs,
 I counted on for the money.
Short night, endless days,
Summer long I continue the chase.
Only way to get money,
In the mountains,
The way life was in my early days.

War

From Missouri to Kentucky,
A stranger made a journey.
In the late 18th century,
Just before the Civil War.
Met his new bride and they married.
Union army was a calling in 1861,
Wife and unborn child would have to wait,
The country was a-calling.
To defend this land,
Some would give it all.
Took his oath at Camp Nelson,
With a long rifle in his hand,
Off he went to defend Camp Wildcat.
Fortress manmade and natural,
The records plainly said.
Known to others as Breast Plate.
On his day during watch,
The rebel soldiers showed their head.
From that distance it looked safe,
Taunting, it could be said.
He climbed on a Brest Plate,
Waving his arms and crowing like a rooster.
A Rebel Soldier shot him dead.
Little boy no father, would he ever see.
John Decker, great-grandfather to me.

In memory of Phillip Franklin Decker.
Death, Camp Wildcat 1861

William Bailey Roberts

From South Carolina to the north,
Near eighteen hundred you made a journey,
To South Kentucky near Tennessee,
For your service you earned a home.
With your wife and family,
As time and children came to be,
 You bore a son of your name.
Many years have come and gone,
With hundreds coming from this family line,
Living throughout this land,
Many were born near where you lay.
One day with ancestors on my mind,
Where I came from I had to know.
By searching endless days and nights,
I learned the story of your life.
There in English graves you all did lay,
I made a wish to honor you I would.
In six generations later,
We gave back your name.
Now, William Bailey Roberts is my grandson.

Family Hands

Log cabin hewed with a broad axe,
Barn built of notched logs.
A picket fence lines the yard.
Split rail fences,
Zigzag the landscape.
Large stone fire place,
Smoke is rising slowly in the morning fog.
Apple tree, Peach tree, and rose bush,
Many flowers blooming,
Dot the springtime landscape.
A horse with a cow and her calf,
Are grazing in a meadow,
 That's near a spring.
Birds of all feathers,
All of nature can be seen.
This is an early home,
Build by family hands.
Aren't you glad you came?

Farm

Took out two more stumps,
On the upper flat today,
Sweat on my brow, my axe in hand,
This is no job for mortal man.
Last year roots caught my plow,
The mules could not pull,
Though hard they tried,
It caused us to let it, "lay by."
This year we plow with hope,
As the year goes by,
There will be corn,
And a field is born.
Mules in the barn,
Chewing on hay,
Mother in kitchen,
Butter milk corn bread.
Tonight I sleep on a straw tick bed,
Feather down pillow, I lay my head.
Tired old body aching toe to head,
Tomorrow I will work in the shed.
Days on an early farm…

Logging

Today we log the upper flats;
Long drag for the mules,
They are tired tonight.
Up and down hills, stretchers in hand.
Liz and Kate, seventeen they stand,
Never was a better team held in my hand.
Log yard in meadow, near the stream,
The mules stop even every log,
As if they knew I'd be there in time.
Drive lines around my neck,
Evening tree in hand,
Pulls me to top like a little plan.
Gee and haw for left and right hand,
Get up and woo is the go and stop plan.
Used both log dogs on most the logs,
Without plowing in the dirt,
Takes all the mules strength,
Pulling the biggest logs!
Corn and oats they will chew on tonight.
Potatoes and beans and corn cakes for me,
Tonight my back and legs will ache.
Logging is hard but I can take.

A Trade

Thirteen, logging was my life,
Gas, hammer and a wedge,
Sometimes we used a pole axe.
Stoke, taught me a trade!
Timber Jack skidder,
Mules and horses,
Stihl chainsaw,
Cross cut and chopping axe.
Loader took, skid pole and cant hook.
The change happens throughout my life.
Logging in the mountains,
Sons and daughters,
Cutting trees was my task.
Always, smile at death every day,
Sometimes wonder why you stay.
Danger in the forest,
Don't allow any city choice,
Logging in your blood,
Sometimes leaving plenty in the woods.
Copper head, rattle snake,
Ticks and brown spiders,
Dangers most worry about.
Set here smiling in my older days,
I beat all the, Widow Makers.

Camping

The camp fires flickering light,
An owl sounds in the distance,
Into the dark of night,
Cool breeze on my skin.
Sound of horses chewing hay,
Lumps in my bed,
Where I now lay!
Stars shine so bright,
Sleep doesn't come,
It is a peaceful night.
Coyote barks in the distance.
The rippling water of a stream,
Everything is quiet,
This is like being in a dream.
Camping and horse riding,
The life lots of us miss.
In back country,
Everything we could wish.

Heart

The curve of their neck,
Wind in your face,
Feet tap out rhythm,
You know they are in place.
With each click of your voice,
You receive their heart,
Power you felt,
Always, from the start;
Heart that is bigger than their body,
Gracefully they glide,
With their greatness,
They allow you to ride.
Together we glide,
As one in flight,
Through the day,
And into the night.
They allow you their spirit,
On endless rides.
A touch on the reins,
You ride horses with pride.

Kind Sugar

Many years we have spent together,
Riding throughout this land,
When we were young,
Pulling sled, cart, and wagon;
In the saddle we had many wars.
We did agree I could be boss,
With a firm but gentle hand,
On and on we would ride through the years,
 I guided you through your fears.
Time would come and go,
As our life together would slow,
Years have changed our dark hair to silver.
The gray on your face,
Like the color on my head.
All these years though I knew you,
Then I truly learned your heart,
While grazing in a meadow,
And a child did approach,
You didn't try and walk away.
Just lowered your gray face head,
And touched your nose to a little hand,
That belongs to a three year old.
All those years we spent together,
I never knew you were so Kind.

Little Doll

The vet lay you down in the barn,
As your eyes watched me,
Over an hour we got to know each other.
Black coat, little head, all legs,
When you rose, chose me over your mother.
Bonds we made would last forever,
As your mother faded, you took her place.
Many years we played together,
Over time you became a horse.
All your fire and energy,
The most I have ever seen,
Your power and passion,
In the saddle you always show.
Kindness barn and children,
Can only come from your mother,
Like you are two horses,
With the fire that's in your heart.
Health and graying days,
I am no match for you.
On your first day into this world,
That little bond we have made,
You allow me to be boss.
For you are, A Little Doll.

A Horse and a Boy

There you stood, looking kind of alone.
Long legs, little head,
Flea bitten, kind of white,
Climbed into saddle, "Go," I said.
It felt like rocking chair,
As I watched your head,
With long stride we traveled,
Back and forth on this road!
Rode so soft, I had to bring you with me,
For a little boys love and make your home.
In my haste to own you,
I never even asked your name.
Pride in his eyes as he looked up with glee,
Marriage made in heaven, it came to be.
They rode all evening on our home road.
Many years would be spent together,
With you and that little boy.
Now you glide the winds at night,
While you rest all day, swatting flies,
Buried under the Old Buckeye Tree.
Yes I did name you and we agreed,
I told him you were, "A Racking Jack."

Ride

Light streaming through the trees,
As the sun, gives way to light.
Birds singing morning songs,
Smoke slowly rising from a campfire.
Breakfast and dishes done,
Now it's time to roll.
Everyone get into a line.
Crossing stream, climbing longest hill,
Like a train rolling slow.
Wheels squeak, chains rattle.
Mountains, trees, dirt roads,
Sound of feet tap out rhythm,
Dust sometimes rises slow.
This is a padded seat,
Place your feet on foot board,
Lean back to relax,
All bound in nature everywhere.
Hold the driveline in your hand.
Although you didn't know,
You just took your first,
Horse and Wagon Ride!

Death of a Stream

Man with his iron rail,
Put a track into a mountain.
Industry must not fail,
Black coal was the gold.
Beautiful stream of trout,
Cold water splash about,
Little children play and sprout,
Mining town sprang up.
Black coal in the cup,
Cold water turning copper,
Little fishes not in water.
Black coal turning streams to copper,
What's happening to the water?
Clear water is not found,
Not a trout around,
All the streams are brown.
Mining town and the children,
Can not to be found.
Brown limestone in a ditch,
Catch pond turning stale,
As if cursed by a witch,
Coal company becoming rich,
You and I with the fish,
Are paying for the ditch!

Fishing and Eagles

Today I visit nature on back country lake,
Fish are biting slow, my time I will take.
Sun shining down on water,
Breeze and white caps you can see,
Reflections of clouds in the water;
Looks like hawks flying all over,
Strange they fly into the water.
Oh look a white cap I do see,
As the Bald Eagle flight crosses me.
Female eagles look like hawk,
I even learned of their butcher block.
Male I knew at first glance,
White hood and tail circling in the sky,
Who cares, if fish don't bite.
Didn't know of my own flight,
Nature has so much to see.
I just need the right place to be,
My hideaway has the eagles,
Watching over me!

Parent

Let me tell you of a person I knew,
I only look up to so few.
One I hold close in my heart,
They taught me to stay true.
The values they placed in me,
Will take me far,
I'll never wonder where they are,
One who always stood so tall!
Never allowing me to fall,
Their voice would calm a room,
Sad they left me so soon.
They live forever in my heart,
Because they taught me do my part.
Now you know and will see,
What A Father is to me.

To Me

Of all the people in my life,
No one has more meaning.
Bonds we made when I was young,
Has stood all these years,
That little boy you rolled his hair,
On those metal clips to get curls.
Held your family together,
Like no other in my time,
You are truly like your mother,
She too was fond of me.
Respect you give me,
Never ask for anything.
Your door is always open,
Just like my own home.
The kindest sister in-law,
That the world will ever see.
All these years putting up with me,
Blessed with two families,
You will always be,
Like a mother, To Me.

Mother Angel

Dark hair and eyes, always glowing,
As the frost of time takes its toll,
Outspoken, with a heart so kind.
With a passion defend your children,
Kept them together all these years.
Hands you work and sew,
Many a quilt you have made,
That kept so many warm.
Holiday's at your house,
These years we always share,
I look forward to every year.
Your door is always open,
To your heart and family,
All these years I have known you,
You have been there for me.
A stronger person I have never known.
If sister in-laws were made in heaven,
There you would surely be,
The Mother Angel,
You would truly be.

A Strong Person

How do I tell of you,
The story of your life,
All the children born,
Throughout your life,
Love, food, and shelter,
Teaching values of life.
Strong will, firm hand,
Showing always be strong,
Work for what you have,
Or all will be gone.
Hours spent over wood stove,
Showing how to cook,
Dusk till dawn work, work.
Large garden, always canning,
Always living off the land.
Low light, you would read at night,
About a bigger plan.
Winters long cold days,
With needle and thread in hand,
You made double sewn quilts,
That kept your children warm.
The values you placed in me,
 All my life never let me down,
They're still here in my heart,
Mother, you never let me down.

Never Go Away

All the many struggles in life,
We face each and every day,
Mothers, fathers, brothers, sisters,
That never seems to stay.
Close friends of the past,
As all are in our thoughts,
On every single day,
Sometimes our many losses,
Seem a large price to pay,
As we continue living,
On these many days;
Aren't, we the lucky ones,
That gets to always stay.
When it comes our time,
We too, will gently go away,
As we live on in memory,
When we are thought of,
On so many days;
Bodies live a short life,
As nothing will last forever.
We watch friends and family,
Slowly just fade away.
Good memories will live forever.
They Never Go Away.

Memories

As we travel forward in time,
Many memories I have seen.
The old world that goes away,
As life changes every day;
People, places, everything,
Never seems to stay the same.
New challenges come our way,
The old ones just go away.
It would be nice,
If more could always stay.
At times in our memory,
That seems so long ago,
From a past better day!
Memories from our past,
Change with world and time,
Never are they left behind.
As we all will change,
To make just who we are,
With Memories, of better days!

Dreams and Hands

All of life's journeys,
The many things I see,
What on earth could it be,
That's waiting next for me.
Adapt to all the changes,
In life as they come and go,
The things I can do,
Like the many scars of life,
That brands me forever more.
Born to be the person,
I know I truly am.
Failing health, problems of many kinds,
Nothing on this earth,
Has stop these hands.
The will my parents gave me,
Will last till the end of time,
With little education they taught me,
You can always make it,
With Dreams and Your Hands!

Dreams

Dreams of a little boy,
Became the will of a man,
As I traveled throughout this land,
Many dreams of all kinds,
Dreams gave me many things.
Skills to do the things I needed,
All the dreams in my past,
Giving me things that would last,
Always have many dreams,
They're as close as your hand.
With dreams everything you can,
Dreams will build a better man.
Dreams, oh what can they see,
Everything you wanted,
All the things you can be.
They were always there for me.

Indian Dan

Life about a different man,
Held so much in his hand,
Many times lost his way,
Were these days here to stay,
One day found his calling,
Ancient blood in his veins,
Wondered what would follow.
Riding horse dark as night,
The wolf became his friend,
Together searching endless dreams,
 In the dark and light.
All of this would come to be,
Everything now in his hand,
Life's new journey all will see,
Finally was his destiny.
Horseman blood flowing red,
Wolf and all of nature in his head,
Buffalo skin for his bed,
Poetry and nature near and far,
Horse and saddle for a car,
Earned his name of the red man,
Family members took a stand,
Called him, Indian Dan!

Find You

The uncle I never knew,
How do I tell of you!
Fireworks and Fourth of July,
Was all I ever knew!
No one ever said or told,
Where you were.
How did you feel,
When they came for you?
In the turning away,
You must have never looked back.
The escape, what did it get,
Was it just more years.
Lessons taught in life,
You did go back,
That little boy you had,
 Did he look for you?
Wonder, was there tears,
We expected you would come.
But there is no coming back,
When you are on the run,
Freeways and internet,
Louisville you now lay,
Family's up north,
We now know who you were,
For I did find you!

Elmer N. Roberts --b 1907

Years and Tears

Damn all these years,
with these many tears.
What have I done?
Had my daughters and my sons,
Like my father's tender years,
I grow older with my fears.
Tears come from the heart,
I learned to live with from the start.
Long I live with this heart,
I see in my family all their fears,
It has happened over many years.
Like my father they have my heart,
One day tears will end for me,
In the end all will see,
The tears are from my heart.
In my end, theirs will start,
For I will be in their heart,
Damn these Years,
With all these Tears!

Mountain Dew

Tall, broad shoulders and a hat,
Deep voice, always polite,
Never showed a temper,
Not even raised your hand,
Stories of your younger days,
I still tell of you.
Logging mules and farming,
All the things that you did,
Those scars on your head,
I know you would never tell.
Riding that old mule behind you,
Down that Obey Hill,
You didn't ever know it,
I pulled his hair,
Is what made him buck.
You can no way ever know,
How much you are missed.
In my life I try to copy you,
Those instructions you gave me,
I know you never knew,
But I can make your Mountain Dew.

Shine

Barrel of water in a shed,
Limestone water, clear as gin,
Now a novelty all have said,
This is how it all begins.

Crystal white sugar in my hand,
Crack corn for the hops,
From this mix I make a stand,
This is a family blend,
Refined by my own hand!

Mixed together it starts to mote,
Little bubbles start to float,
Sweet to sour is the goal,
Mash is the closer phrase.
Moonshine whisky is the crave,

Now it's working to the phase.
Limestone water turning brown,
Clear whisky dripping down,
Brown white oak like charcoal,
Is waiting in a mason jar.

Distilling whisky violates law,
ATF wonders where you are,
Not allowing it in jar,
Good cover will go far.
Kentucky bourbon is not so far,
Now the world will see 100 years,
Luther's whisky made it to DC.

New Life

As one travels through time,
Things one did and didn't do,
The many stories one could tell,
Faces in memories we can still see.
We have won and lost so many times.
Crumbled dreams of the past,
Brought new dreams to life,
Nothing is good the way it is,
Always there's a better way.
Next fascination will appear.
Will not stop until it's done,
Task completed it means the end,
Now a new one can begin.
The roads of life we live on,
Have a lot of curves,
Many times it finds you,
Coming back with New Life!

Who You Are

Have you ever wondered,
Who you really are?
Why you do the things you do,
That makes you just you.
Mix of blood and environment,
It does determine you.
Endless days searching,
As the way they went.
Always question everything,
Never knowing why,
Many times with fears and tears,
Time and time we had to try.
The many mix you have,
Proves you are like no other,
Strong will, always push you,
It's no secret, you are you.

Spirit

The sun is slowly rising,
Out over Pilot Rock,
Let's go play on the cliffs,
Gliding hill and valley,
Maybe we can play all day.
Oh look down the valley,
I can race you to that gate.
The wind in that pine tree,
It woke me last night,
Grandpa had to put me back in bed,
This velvet grass is so soft,
Stone kind of hurt my head.
This little hill,
Makes a wonderful home,
Tonight we will travel,
To the old home place,
Over the upper ridge,
Where we can spend some time,
Just playing in shadows,
Of moon light,
Under the Cedar Trees!

Forever

Oh brother, can you see,
Living in the mountains,
In our early years,
Hills and cliffs to climb and play,
Didn't we fight every day?
Forest fires, oh how did they start!
Fields and garden we had to work,
Spring, walk behind the plow,
Dig in corn, sprout off stumps,
Where are they now, can you see?
Hunt at night, with lantern light,
With old yard dog,
Remember his first squirrel,
Old man showed how it's done,
Smoke and twisted out of tree.
Running through the mountains,
In our early years, bound our hearts,
For these many years,
Sled and wagon ride, many a mud hole,
Ride horse and mule like cowboys.
Returning to these hills,
Our spirits will forever travel,
Running with the mountain winds,
As we did in younger days,
We will Forever more.

Turning Away

When you would not stay,
For nothing you threw it away,
How many scars could it leave?
For years I never understood,
The pain in our heart,
In the lines on our face,
How could it be!
That the emptiness we felt,
How everything meant so little,
Nothing in this life can erase.
When you look back at this world,
Feelings and dreams just go away.
Time and past just wither away,
Life has changed to shadows,
Changed forever of a world of the past.
In time it all goes away.
Your world will never stay,
All because of your, turning away!

Life's Door

This ever changing world,
Pushes us through another door,
It's hard to explain,
From a child from a mountain top,
To one from a big city block,
Life keeps pushing hard.
We see so much change,
Happiness, sadness coming back,
Pushing us through,
City life, lights, bars, and cars,
The little children with eyes so bright,
Jobs and new houses,
How many have we had, one can't see,
All my life they change for me.
Opening and closing throughout our time,
All the faces, too far to see,
Many times a heavy hand.
Where have we tread, or do we go?
Look out a window, or step into a yard,
Ride in a car, or walk along a river,
Look at the ground, to the sky,
Your families face, lover, or a friend,
How many Doors have you seen?

Time and Years

The way you pass the test of time,
Is always held in your hand,
Our moments shared, and time spent,
Turning into the days went.
Changing days into months,
The sound of voice, A touch of your hand,
Has earned my trust no goal in mind,
Honesty and devotion is easy to see,
Eyes with beauty with emotions,
Hands of kindness are there for me.
The smile on your face,
My heart in place,
As the months turns into years,
It's so easy anyone can see.
I wish I had of known you,
In my younger years,
You have out lasted all the others.
All these many Years!

Cold

Many years ago
I thought we would belong
Although, could we have a life
Gave my heart to you then
I know I never got it back
The life that we have made
It will take me to my grave
This little beat that's now in my heart
Is probably because it's so cold
Feelings for what we had
The emptiness that remains in my soul
The winters wind and snow
No matter how hard it blows
Only my skin will feel it
For empty hearts can never heal
Because they are so Cold.

Old Fred

Once going down Hurricane Road,
I met Old Fred.
Sam's feet were glowing red,
Said, "Her brakes was a dragging,"
Mop Head's hair blowing in the wind,
Kale, had milk on her chin.
Fred has passed so many times,
With a breath of life,
He will always return,
Scars of a rough life,
Easy anyone can see,
Old Fred will always go,
Just place your feet,
Through the Floor!

Old Mop Head

From the time you were born,
Laying in my floor,
Frozen in time with a camera,
There would be many more.
Your life came about,
 Always living everywhere!
One long cold winter's day,
Whiney didn't want to play,
We made foot prints in the snow.
Pack of smokes made you boast,
Down in water tank said: "to smoke,"
Head was poking out like a ground hog.
Curls came slow on your head,
Covering up your ears,
Blabber mouth, pretty face,
Everyone must truly love.
Time I cherish the most,
While playing in a field,
You walked up to Old Sugar,
She kindly lowered her head,
Touching your gentle little hand,
With her gray nose!
Your curls have earned your name.
Pa, pa truly loves you,
Said you were, "Old Mop Head."

Little Petals

As I started out in life,
Always cared for many flowers,
One day got a rose, added beauty to my life.
Time passed I got another,
Before long got two more,
Now I had four beautiful roses,
Care for them and watch them grow.
One day I watched my roses go away.
Caring for my roses would not be of my say,
Petals on my roses would wither as they grew.
Then I got two more roses to hold in my hands,
 Care for them with my time,
Many times I held them in my hands.
Kept them close to my heart,
With tender loving care,
Growing into beautiful rosebush,
The years would show.
Now there are beautiful rose petals,
That I hold in my hands.
Oh, did I tell you of my roses,
They are of so many kinds,
And their little Petals,
They are so, so fine.

Day

Of the many poems I could write of you,
And all the many things that I can say,
What should be said, on this special day?
Love has no boundaries,
 On what one should say,
All these many years,
 Filled with empty spaces,
Time has never taken it away,
I have lived with this forever,
So, now it's time for me to say.
It was all my intention,
To love you all the way,
Time and years and all these tears,
Have never taken you away,
Only thing I need do now,
Upon this special day,
 Is I know I will always love you,
Until that final Day.

You and Me

As you entered into this world,
I had no book on how it goes.
Time has taught us all,
Have to walk before you fall.
All came first has paid a price,
For the ones that would follow.
Things each never had,
Was not a father at your side!
We never had but two rules,
I can't remember one of them.
Respect and honor was our goal,
Rules of older days one could say,
What you say was your word.
Of the many things we know,
The many lessons you taught me,
Only our eyes can truly see.
Took my place as I belonged,
As each of you know,
How you all gave me strength.
Today I smile as I watch you,
For there looking back is me.

Stay

Many years ago,
Added you to my life,
Although I did not know,
How that road would go.
All these years I have tried.
The honor in our children,
I know will always stay,
They have given me the will,
To live and have good days!
Though you went away,
Emptiness of the soul,
Has seemed to always stay,
Although you are not here,
On these lonely days,
In my heart and memory,
I think of you every day.
From the many years away,
You will always stay.

Person

Let me tell of a person I know,
Never would I let go,
Always stands out in a crowd,
One who always give their all,
Never falter, never fall.
Never waiting for their call,
One that's always there,
A person that is tried and true,
Who's always standing tall!
This person gives it all,
Never allowing me to wait,
The values they have,
Their trust in me,
Everything in life,
I could wish it to be,
True to do their part,
Comes straight from the heart,
Now you can clearly see,
  The values I have in you.

Look Up To You

On all these many days,
Although you went away,
Even when it broke my heart,
When you could no longer stay,
Things you gave and taught,
Forever binds my mind and heart.
Keep you close all these years,
Helped me through my many fears,
The way you were there for me,
In time I will join up with you,
But for now I will have to wait.
Though you are still here every day,
I will make the entire world to see,
How I do Look Up To You.

Burn Out

Look into your soul,
The way you live,
What have you become.
Does the price you pay,
Worth your time of the day,
Puppet world you live in,
Sell your soul for a life,
What on earth you get back.
Know so little of your world,
Blinded not by light,
Everything's not as they look.
As your ray of light,
Blinds all your sight,
Like a glowing sun,
One day will Burn Out.

Sister

All the years together,
You and I have spent,
Growing up with your brothers,
Could not be heaven sent.
Mother stayed close to you,
Cleaning house, cook on woodstove.
Working garden and her flowers,
Even taught you how to sew;
Married young with little children,
Makings of a hard life,
We took separate roads.
As our lives would go,
Always there for a brother,
A kind and gentle voice,
When my times got rough,
And I didn't know where to go,
Many times I used your shoulder.
Our parents bound our heart,
Proud you are my sister,
Forever from the start.

Last Wagon Ride

Bell Farm and wagon riding,
My first journey into the past,
We made a friendship that last.
Mules and wagon, Mack and Ely,
Next time we met evening tree in hand,
Mule logging was your plan.
Years of riding, sharing stories,
Camping many times,
All the miles we traveled
While holding our lines in hands.
Time and illness took its toll,
As you faded it would go slow.
Once you told a story of a friend,
As your emotions showed,
Of a last wagon ride,
Family and friends came together,
On how it would be,
Hurst stopped at the church in the trees,
As we placed you in the wagon,
Behind old Mack and Ely's evening tree.
Like our first wagon ride,
We followed you down that road,
To your resting place,
As we took our Last Wagon Ride!

Hands

Let me tell of a heart,
Only you will truly know,
You held in your hands so, so long ago.
Pushing forward as the seeds we sow,
How on earth could it be replaced?
Time can never start to erase,
Devoted to a love going nowhere,
Everything has to go away,
We didn't think our life together,
Would somehow always stay,
The way it is when hearts do part.
Tiny little hands we made,
They have took your place,
You're chasing many dreams,
Has placed you where you are.
Only now my love,
My Hands alone hold my heart.

Stand

On the day you were born,
Didn't know you belong,
Made a pledge I would,
Hold you in my arms,
Bond you to my heart.
Years would come and go,
At times, it was a hard life.
With me guiding those little hands.
You followed in my footsteps,
I taught you everything I could.
Like I do my father,
You now look up to me.
The years and tears,
We have went through,
Molding those little hands,
It has made you a bigger man.
Proud to be your father,
Made us better men.
For you my son,
I'll always Stand.

Me

From the day you were born,
Pride and joy in my heart,
Making me a proud man,
Love, guide and teach,
Make everything in your reach.
Family became divided,
Life became a bigger task,
Held your little hands,
I taught you things to last.
Although we did not know,
How far your life would go,
Becoming the smartest person,
I could ever wish.
Things done and learned,
Everything it could be.
The education in your head,
Gives you things I cannot do,
Many places you will see.
Graying in time and years,
Everything I want to be,
For today, my son,
You are just like me.

Destiny

Did you ever wondered,
About fate or destiny!
Can one ever understand,
All of life's changes that we see,
That's not being really planned.
Falling into perfect place,
That's never by your own hand.
Skills that we learn,
Pales in what we know,
Roads where we travel,
On and on they seem to go.
One truly has no limit,
It's amazing what we can,
All the things that you touch,
Truly has a bigger plan.
Traveling on not knowing,
Pieces falling into perfect place,
Never a word to be said,
Everything in life that's Destiny.

Little Hands

When you were a little girl,
You were everything to my world,
Tiny hand in mine,
With little legs, you chased after me.
The many things that came about,
 Little would we know,
That the many roads we travel,
Not knowing where they go.
For your love and support,
I gave you everything I knew.
We work together, farm and logging,
Taking care of each other,
Like a father and daughter can.
Make sure you know me,
Has been my biggest plan,
While holding close to that little hand,
You never had to look for me.
Years have gave us respect,
We now truly understand.
For today, my daughter,
You hold my heart,
In those Little Hands!

Miss You

I wonder if you miss me,
Your world of run, run,
I always wanted to see,
What our life could be.
Blood flowing in our veins,
Bound us forever,
You are of my body,
We truly are the same.
Years of our time together,
Has bound our heart,
Body, mind, and spirit,
Always has from the start.
Walk proud all your life,
Never to be looking back.
The way you live,
It's taken you from me.
I wonder if you are near,
Days that we do share,
Means everything to me,
For today, I am Missing You.

Sorrow

Life can be filled with sorrows,
Everything is not always grand,
Wear your heart on your sleeve,
Then your life you can truly see.
Many a failure one can have,
Times that's so, so sad,
Little children have gone away,
Not a bed you wish to lay.
New faces in your world,
Now giving you a new life,
Starting over its been said,
Again, finds you fighting for a life.
Little children that's like no other,
Like all the sorrow in your heart.
With pain and sorrow make your start,
Teach your children to be smarter.
With the tears of a heart!
Now you lay alone instead,
In the end you made your bed.
Wished you missed all the sorrow,
Didn't know what would follow.
Now you are standing proud,
You have your life in your hands.
Now true to your heart.
Should have been from the start!

Across the Pond

There once was a young lad,
That went fishing with his Dad.
 On almost, every single day!
Learned fishing the old way,
Like fishing always goes,
On every single day,
Wondering along the pond,
Each going their separate way,
Until they were almost gone,
Only to be seen at a distance.
Time has made a bigger bond.
Anyone can really see,
Reason why they can't fish,
They are just across,
A Bigger Pond!

Hard Times

From the beginning of our time,
My life has been about you.
Struggles of our every day,
Have never gotten in our way!
Though never did you know,
When I knew not where to go,
You carried me through hard times.
The strength that you gave me,
Determine who we are today.
What I'm really trying to say:
Like in our past days and time,
Where you carried me over mine,
 I would never leave you behind,
For I will always be there for you,
Through all your, Hard Times.

Grandson

As we sit here with you next to me,
That little hand touching mine,
Wonder what those eyes can really see,
Like a ghost from the past,
I have saw this somewhere before.
That big old name we placed on you,
It will forever make you strong,
Everywhere you go.
The entire world it will show,
For the ones before you,
They will teach you well,
All throughout your life,
Everything you hope to become,
The son, anyone could want you to be.
And today all the world,
Can look and truly see,
Just what a grandson,
Can really be.

A Soldier

As she wrapped her little arms,
Around your neck and face,
I would say your heart did race,
When you look into her face,
She didn't know for sure,
Daddy's is going off some place.
My camera cannot show,
Caught in time, and frozen in space,
The strains on ones heart and soul,
Time will slowly start to erase.
Bound to a duty for a life,
Five years to get to this place.
Voids in the heart and years,
In a little time it will erase,
For again, there will be,
A really happy face,
For a home coming will take place.

As Memories Fade

Today I can see what you have become
In our journey all the things we have done
Sacrifice were made
Just to make who we are
Like the morning fog in the mountains
With a fading memory
All will go away
As our memory slowly fades
You will know that
So too will your face
Traveling on in empty space
Life will show all its scars
But today, I thought I was Dad.

KENTUCKY PRIDE

Kentucky born and bred,
we inherited our southern ways.
At UK, the banners wave,
Derby town, Thoroughbreds, break from the gate.
On southern lakes a boat ride,
Back country camping, horse or wagon ride.
We make our Bourbon, and call it Tea.
Its all about our southern ways,
always stand for what we said,
we look you in the eyes,
And never turn our heads.
For you will never see,
no fear in our eyes.
Just looking back in memories,
my life has many times,
brought me to my knees.
I always survived somehow.
Nothing I have ever wanted,
that I could not do,
I always have my own ways.
I believe that when I die,
the angels are going to cry,
they will bury my body
before they bury my Pride.
~ Cas Roberts 2012

Reality Show: on Discovery Channel

The Blue Grass Boys

How about them Blue Grass Boys!
Spring time in the mountains
It's time to grow.
On Discovery Channel they got a show
Tell the world on how its done.
A Ghost truck, to make a break
Cameo camper, with all at stake.
Freddie try's to run the Rabbit down
Old Cass, just stuck up a tree
Not one friend can he see
Left behind for all to be free.
Now the show has hit's the air
Blue Grass Boys are the star.
Now to handle all this fame
Freddie is searching near and far
Old Red hit's the air
The Rabbit's on the run
Cass is having all the fun
While Pony Boy,
"Just looks good in Orange!"

When Darkness Closes In

Streaks of sun light filtering through the clouds
as darkness closes in.
I watch the evening change to total darkness
as calmness surrounds me.
Laying here in total darkness
A light breeze is softly touching my skin.

I look up into a turbulent nighttime sky,
Watching clouds drift
in shadows across the horizon
blocking out the moon and stars.
Ghostly shadows move endless flight
slowly, across dangerous skies.

I drift to a different time
As memories tumble inside my head
I close my eyes, but it doesn't go away.
Remembering the softness of your voice
and the gentle touch of your hand
with moon light glowing on your skin.

It's all just shadows from long ago
when you walk away and you're alone again.
Then the night begins to fade
As the turbulence goes away
 to only return on another day.
You're playin' to win
But you are losing just the same.

The Hands of Time

As the hands of time slowly tick away
The things that will be missed
As they pass upon their way
Thoughts of all the roads
That one has traveled
Just seams as morning fog
Like the sun always takes it away
Journeys take one many places
But they only last a short time
For nothing can last forever
As the hands of time takes all away.

Betrayal

Through betrayal
with every twist and turn.
Satin's little helper
is who you have become.

It's all about control,
believing you will win.

But, those we love
don't just go away.
They always walk beside us
all the way.

May god bless
all the little children.
That doesn't ever
get to have a say.

Liberty Michelle with Papaw Cas,

Up on that horse for a walk through the grass,
Holding onto the reigns all smiles, no pains,
These were the best out of all of the days.

Ezekiel Jude with Pap aw Cas,
Right broken arm, but one happy mood.
Horseshoes clunk in', feet just a'thumpin,
So much excitement, his heart was a'pumpin.

And once Mr. Big gin,
Now Mr. Michael Cas,
The bond we share, no one else has.
And I don't know it all,
But this much is true.
When I grow up,
I wanna be like you.

Mister Sun

Mister Sun, Mister Sun,
When are you coming down?
Down on the mountain top,
Down the glen.
Mister Sun, Mister Sun,
Why don't you come on down?
Out in the fields,
To play with men.
The reeds in the current,
Are rippling.
The river is wind'in,
To and fro.
Mister Sun, mister Sun,
Hurry along or
you will miss the song.
Mister Sun, Mister Sun.

Contracted, to music,
Sheet and Deno 78 records
Jan 1, 1962
With, Music City Songcrafters
Nashville TN
The art work of an eleven year old boy.
Author: Cas Roberts in 1961

Magic Love

As I sit thinking of you
A shadow of your face
Tumbles, inside my head
The memories of your voice
Oh, so warms my heart.

Just the touch of your hand
As I gaze into your eyes
The soft caress of your lips
With your breath upon my skin
And feel the warmth of your body
As your heart beats close to mine.

Only that can only quiet this desire
That's burning within my soul
Oh, I so miss our times
While you are so far away
I just want to be inside your heart
And hold you safe in my arms.

Today, I Remember Yesterday.

Today, while I am setting here in my barn brings back memories of past days in time. I take a look down the bottoms along the creek as I see the corn field, and scan the soybeans in the five acres field near my property. The old riding horse that is standing near to me, is silently swatting flies, while I listen to her sounds of chewing on hay. Today has a cool breeze, as my mind drift to another place in time and I was a young lad.

Drifting back in my thoughts, I remember plodding barefoot through the dirt field behind the horse and plow, with the cool feeling of the earth upon the skin of my feet. The work in the fields and gardens of those days still leaves a smile on my face. I also think about all the times on hot summer days as kids, my brothers and I with friends, we all went swimming in the old creek. Ah, times are changing, and as they have passed and I am getting older, today, I remember yesterday. ~Cas Roberts

Be sure to check out our other books at Amazon.com
As Country As It Gets, Short stories from Appalachia

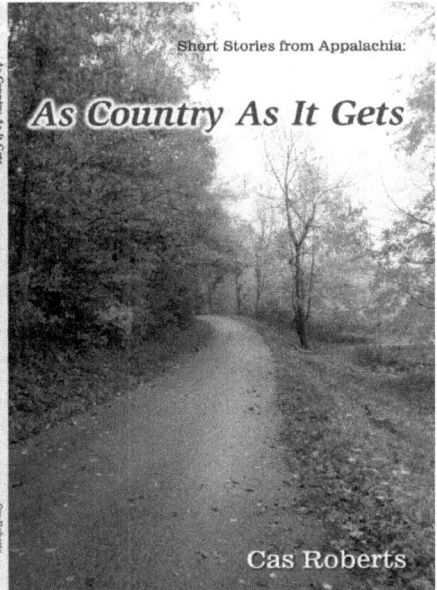

Short Stories from Appalachia:

As Country As It Gets

Cas Roberts sixty-five yrs. Old is retired and resides in Lincoln Co., Kentucky. Cas was born and raised having nine siblings in the mountains of Wayne Co., Kentucky. At an early age, he worked the log and saw mill trade. Two marriages resulted in six children. Cas says, "Appalachia is my roots."

Take a journey with Cas as he shares his personal experiences and memories through his stories of a preserved way of life where it is. "As Country as it Gets;" an era where his Appalachian heritage and upbringing lifestyle is preserved for many generations to see through his work. The Old World way of life, with wild ginseng hunting, mule logging, horses, mules and wagon riding, professional coon hunting, and yes, even the fine art of moonshiner is also a part of his heritage.

Cas Roberts

www.ingramcontent.com/pod-product-compliance
Lightning Source LLC
Chambersburg PA
CBHW060652030426
42337CB00017B/2568